LIFE AND TIMES IN
THE VIKING
WORLD

KINGFISHER

KINGFISHER

Kingfisher Publications Plc
New Penderel House
283–288 High Holborn
London WC1V 7HZ
www.kingfisherpub.com

Based on material first published in the Sightseers series
by Kingfisher Publications Plc 2000

This edition first published by Kingfisher Publications Plc 2007
2 4 6 8 10 9 7 5 3 1

1TR/0607/TIMS/(MA)/14OMA/C

Written and edited by: Sheila Clewley, Julie Ferris, Conrad Mason
Consultant: Robin Allan
Production controller: Aysun Ackay
DTP manager: Nicky Studdart

Illustrations by: John James and Kevin Maddison

A CIP catalogue record for this book
is available from the British Library.

ISBN 978 0 7534 1559 7 (paperback)
ISBN 978 0 7534 1628 0 (hardback)

Printed in China

Contents

The Viking world

The Vikings lived in Scandinavia, in northern Europe. They were great seafarers, traders and explorers, and won a ferocious reputation for their daring raids on other countries. They also travelled as far afield as Greenland, North America and North Africa. The cold climate and long winters of Scandinavia bred hardy, courageous tribes who lived together on farms or in fortified trading communities.

▽ Viking raids began long before 1010CE, when this book is set. The Vikings were a tough people. Fighting and bloodshed were part of their culture, and traditional Norse religion even involved human sacrifice.

△ The three great trading centres of the Viking world were Ribe, Birka and Hedeby. The largest of these, Hedeby, was a coastal town in Denmark. It was well fortified – 10m-high ramparts protected it from attacks by land.

The first Viking raid was on Lindisfarne, Scotland, in 793CE. The Vikings plundered the monastery, stealing treasures.

Viking explorers reached Russia in around 855CE and brought back all kinds of goods for trading.

In 874CE the Vikings established a settlement in Iceland. The inhospitable land made life hard for the pioneers.

There were three distinct groups in the Viking world – Swedes, Norwegians and Danes. However, they all spoke the same language (Old Norse) and had very similar customs. The Viking population was scattered sparsely across huge areas of land. Most regions were ruled over by rich and powerful kings or chieftains, while ordinary Vikings earned a living as fishermen, farmers or traders.

▷ Seafaring was so important that dead Vikings were often buried in boats. Graves were sometimes laid out in the shape of a ship, showing that death was a voyage into the unknown.

In 907CE the Vikings attacked the wealthy city of Constantinople. However, they failed to capture it.

The Viking Leif Eriksson explored Vinland in North America in around 1000CE and established a settlement.

By 1000CE Christianity had spread far into the Viking world and even became the official religion in Iceland.

Viking travel

△ The frightening carved figureheads were removed from ship prows when sailing in friendly waters so that local gods were not upset.

▷ Navigation was a problem on long voyages. Sailors looked at the sun and stars to work out their position at sea. They had tools to measure the height of the sun.

Most Vikings lived on the coast and travelled everywhere they could by boat. Their ships were sturdy enough to cross oceans, and had flat bases to allow them to sail along shallow rivers. However, long sea voyages became difficult in the harsh winter. Inland roads were little more than rough, muddy tracks through steep terrain.

Raiding boats, or longships, were also known as 'serpents of the sea'. This was because their prows were often decorated with a carving of a terrifying creature. Vikings believed that the monster would frighten enemy gods.

▽ Merchant vessels were called knarrs, and were broader and slower than the speedy longships. Goods from distant lands were unloaded on the shore and taken to the nearest settlement for trade.

Vikings travelled between trading centres by foot, wagon or on horseback. They usually went in large, armed groups so that they would not be attacked and robbed. While sailing became harder in the winter, inland travel became much easier. Mud froze over, making the ground firmer, and skates, skis and sledges could be used on the ice and snow. Iron spikes were nailed into horses' hooves to help grip the ice.

△ Travellers used skates to cross frozen lakes and rivers. These were made from horse, ox or deer bone which was smoothed flat on the underside. Wooden skis and a stick helped people to slide over the snow.

▽ Sailors used oars if the wind was unfavourable, but ships could travel more than twice as fast when using their sails.

Clothing

Viking clothes were simple but practical. Men wore linen undershirts, belted woollen tunics and trousers, while women wore long, loose dresses and full-length aprons fastened with brooches. Vegetable dyes, decorative borders and embroidery were used to brighten the hard-wearing clothes. In the winter people wore thick wool or fur cloaks to keep warm.

▽ Married Viking women covered their hair with a scarf as a sign of modesty.

◁ The richest Vikings wore finely decorated jewellery made of gold, while ordinary people had items made out of bronze or silver.

Both men and women wore armrings, bracelets, necklaces, brooches and rings made by local craftsmen. Heavy metal rings called torques were worn around the neck. Many people also had amulets, special items of jewellery which were supposed to bring good luck.

▷ Viking women often hung useful items from the brooches they used to fasten their aprons. These included sewing tools, combs, purses and keys.

▽ Men fastened their cloaks on the right shoulder so that their sword arm was not restricted by the heavy material. Warm cloaks for winter were made out of bear, seal or squirrel furs.

Clothing was made by Viking women, who wove their own fabric and made things for themselves and their families. Sewing implements were made from wood or bone. In the largest trading towns people could buy silk from Asian merchants. This was very fashionable but delicate and extremely expensive. It was usually worn only on special occasions.

△ Women wore their long hair tied in a knot at the back. Men had beards and drooping moustaches. They were kept trim and tidy, and some Vikings even plaited their beards.

Both men and women wore slip-on leather shoes made from goatskin or cattle hide. The soles had no heels, so they wore out quickly. Men usually hung their sword and purse from a leather belt, while women wore their dresses loose and unbuckled.

Food and drink

Viking families produced their own food. Their farms and cattle provided them with a steady supply of grain, vegetables and meat. Meanwhile, the rivers and seas yielded a huge variety of fresh fish. Food was usually plentiful but meat and fish had to be smoked or salted in the summer so that they could be eaten in the winter months.

▷ Vikings ate twice a day – in the morning and in the evening. Meals were substantial and often included several large courses.

▷ People usually ate off their laps, cutting their food with knives and eating with their fingers from wooden bowls and plates. Tables and stools were set up for special occasions.

▷ All cooking was done by the women of the house. They used a large metal cauldron suspended over the fire by a chain that was fixed to the roof of the longhouse (a Viking home).

◁ Vikings hunted for their meat. As well as wild boar and reindeer, they also caught large sea mammals such as seals, walruses and even whales.

Ordinary people ate meat broths and stews, barley bread and salt fish, and drank ale or mead. Vegetables and dairy produce such as milk and cheese were also important parts of the Viking diet. All kinds of fish were eaten, including cod, herring, shellfish and eels. The richest Vikings feasted on seabirds, mutton, wild boar and gull's eggs, and even elk and reindeer meat.

Trade

The Vikings established extensive trading routes all over Europe, and their merchants travelled far to sell goods such as timber, amber and animal furs. Viking market towns offered exotic goods from foreign lands, as well as fresh food and local produce. Piracy was common, so trading towns were well-defended.

△ Large towns minted silver coins. These examples from Hedeby are decorated with a ship design.

A market town such as Hedeby had crowded streets lined with craftsmen's houses and stalls offering a wide range of goods. Most merchants traded by bartering (exchanging goods of equal value), but by the year 1000CE coins had started to be used in the larger settlements.

◁ Many towns had large slave markets. People were captured on raids and sold as slaves throughout the Viking world.

△ As well as repairing tools and weapons, blacksmiths made a wide variety of iron goods including swords, pans and keys.

Different parts of the Viking world were famed for trading in particular goods. The Norwegians supplied timber, Greenland and Iceland traded in seal oil and woollens, and iron ore came from Sweden. The Vikings also imported wine from France, slaves and fur from Russia, and silk and spices from Constantinople and Persia. The goods were transported by sea or overland by river.

△ Market towns were full of craftsmen, from blacksmiths to weavers and antler-carvers. Many of them worked outside because Viking houses let in very little daylight.

Homes

A Viking home, or longhouse, had just one enormous room in which the whole family ate, worked and slept. They shared the house with guests, servants and slaves, and in the winter months even brought in animals to keep them safe from the cold. Very important Vikings had small rooms of their own.

▷ Longhouses usually had no windows. It was more important for the house to be warm than for it to be well lit.

◁ Houses in towns were much smaller than the big longhouses in the country. This was because there was less space available.

The sides of a Viking longhouse were lined with earth platforms where people slept. There was very little furniture. Most homes had a table, a few low stools and wooden chests with locks to hold belongings.

△ Women spent a lot of time in the longhouse. As well as looking after the children, they prepared and cooked food, wove cloth and made clothes.

▽ In the winter, cattle were kept in a pen at the back of the longhouse. Pet dogs scavenged for leftover food on the ground.

△ Vikings kept clean by bathing every Saturday in a sauna. This was a small building near the longhouse, where water was thrown on red-hot stones to produce cleansing steam.

At the centre of every longhouse was a huge fireplace edged with stones. It was a vital source of heat and was also used to cook food. As there was no chimney, smoke escaped through a small hole in the roof.

△ To maximize space in the longhouse, bedding was rolled up during the day. Important household members slept nearest to the fire, where it was warmest.

Viking warriors

▽ Almost all warriors worked as farmers or fishermen for most of the year. Every man had a chest on the longship in which to store armour and weapons. This doubled up as a seat when he was rowing. There could be up to 60 longships on a raid.

Viking warriors were among the most feared fighters in Europe. In the spring and summer they set sail in longships to attack the treasure-filled monasteries of England, Ireland and France. Some Vikings fought as professional mercenaries, offering their services to whoever would pay them the most money. The most deadly warriors were the 'Berserkers', who never wore armour.

▽ Longships were also used for sea battles. After firing arrows and throwing spears at the enemy, the longships drew close and hand-to-hand fighting began.

Viking boys were trained to fight from a very young age. They practised fighting with blunt, wooden weapons, and were only allowed to use a proper weapon when they became an adult. In battle Vikings fought hard to protect their jarl (chieftain). If he was killed, the other warriors were expected to carry on fighting until they were all dead.

▷ Some pieces of armour, such as this helmet, were decorated with elaborate patterns and images. This showed that the owner was rich or important.

◁ An iron helmet and a wooden shield provided protection. Most fighters also wore a padded leather tunic, and wealthy warriors had chain mail. Axes and spears were popular weapons, but double-edged swords were prized above all. They were passed down from father to son and even given names.

A Viking feast

All Vikings held feasts for their friends and relatives, but the biggest were those organised by the local jarls (chieftains). These were held to celebrate victories and special occasions or to make the host look generous. The jarl's great hall was lined with benches, the finest tableware was brought out and everyone dressed in their best clothing and jewellery.

▽ Most Vikings served ale or mead at a feast, but the jarl would usually provide wine. Jarls who particularly wanted to impress their guests would host a feast in mid-winter, when food was at its most scarce.

▷ The most important part of a feast was the drinking. Women were allowed to serve food and wine, but had to leave if the guests became too drunk and rowdy.

◁ Servants regularly refilled the drinking horns. A full horn had to be drunk at once, as it could not be put down without spilling all of the wine.

▷ Seating arrangements at a feast were often hierarchical – important guests had the honour of sitting next to the jarl. Sometimes seating was decided by drawing lots.

◁ The skald would often tell poems about the jarl's success in battle. Viking verse used special phrases to describe familiar things – a battle was a 'game of iron'. Occasionally guests were called upon to join in and recite a verse themselves.

Professional poets (skalds) were hired to entertain guests at a feast. They recited poems about famous battles or events in Viking history. Poems were passed from generation to generation, and were never written down. The skald often made up some verses, including one or two that praised the host.

Leisure time

Vikings worked hard and had little spare time. What free time they had was often spent practising their fighting techniques. Their games and pastimes were very physical and violent, so that they would stay tough and fit for battle. When relaxing, Vikings enjoyed inventing riddles and swapping insults.

▽ Vikings loved to gamble, and placed bets on the outcome of spectator sports such as horse fighting and wrestling.

△ A favourite spectator sport was horse fighting. Two stallions battled together, egged on by their owners who beat them with sticks to make them fight more viciously.

Wrestling, juggling with knives and fencing were some of the dangerous sports enjoyed by Vikings. Even swimming competitions were bloodthirsty, with competitors trying to drown their opponents to win.

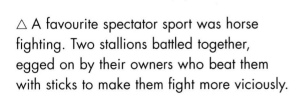

△ The Vikings did enjoy some quieter forms of entertainment. Board games were popular, and the most widely played was hnefatafl. It was a game of strategy, similar to chess.

▽ Wrestling contests took place in the open air. Spectators gathered round the fighters, standing close so that they could get a good view.

△ In most wrestling matches the competitors had to pin their opponent to the ground to win.

Vikings were very competitive in sports, and boys began training at an early age. Winning was a matter of honour, and sportsmen would stop at nothing to be victorious. It was not unusual for a wrestling contest to end in serious injury, or even in death.

Temples and worship

Vikings were very tolerant of different religions. Their own traditional Norse religion involved the worship of many gods, but the three principal ones were Odin (god of war and wisdom), Thor (god of thunder) and Frey (god of nature and fertility). By 1000CE, many of the Vikings had converted to Christianity.

△ Christian churches were built all over the Viking world. Called 'stave' churches, they were made of wood and had tall, triangular roofs.

▽ According to Norse religion, a Viking who had died in battle was taken to Valhalla (the god Odin's great hall), where he feasted and drank with his fellow warriors forever.

Norse worship normally took place in the open air. However, there was a great temple to the gods at Uppsala in Sweden. Every nine years a special festival was held there, during which a sacrifice was made to the gods of nine males of every living thing, from dogs and horses to human beings.

△ In a traditional chief's funeral, his body was placed on a boat with all of his possessions, and the boat was set alight.

▷ There were no priests in Norse religion. Instead, local chiefs led worship and made sacrifices.

▷ The temple at Uppsala housed huge statues of Odin, Thor and Frey.

23

Viking colonies

As well as exploring, Vikings set up thriving colonies in distant lands. In 874CE they journeyed north and settled in Iceland. Greenland was discovered at some time between 980–990CE by Erik the Red, a Viking who was outlawed from Iceland for manslaughter. Although cold and barren, it was named Greenland to entice other Vikings to move there!

▽ Longhouses in Iceland and Greenland were covered with peat and sunk into the ground to protect against the cold.

Vikings settled only in the most habitable parts of Iceland and Greenland. As well as tending to their crops and livestock, they traded with other parts of the Viking world. They exported furs, hides, ropes, falcons and oil, and imported corn, iron and timber. Timber was vital as few trees grew in the extreme climate.

24

▽ At the centre of the althing was the Lögberg – 'Law Rock'. People stood on the rock to deliver speeches and judgements.

◁ Erik the Red's son Leif travelled west from Greenland and landed in Newfoundland. He named it Vinland. Unlike the other colonies, it had a good climate and fertile land. However, the native Americans put up strong resistance and the Vikings did not stay there for very long.

▷ The Vikings of Greenland lived so far to the north that they had continuous sunshine in summer and continuous darkness in winter.

Every summer the Vikings of Iceland held an 'althing' – a huge meeting at which laws were agreed, important issues were discussed and disputes were settled. 'Things' were held all over the Viking world, but they were mostly very small and dealt with local issues.

Eastern trade routes

The Vikings established extensive trade routes and settlements to the east and south. The native Slavs referred to the Vikings as 'Rus', and the area in which they settled became the country of Russia. In the far south was the greatest city of all – Constantinople, the largest and most powerful city in Europe.

△ Vikings travelled east by boat along the vast network of rivers. When they had to change river or travel overland, they used logs to roll the boat over the ground.

▽ Rus merchants set up trading posts along the rivers. The settlement at Kiev emerged as the most important. It was used as a base for trade with Constantinople.

△ The Varangian Guard were a band of Viking warriors who served the emperor of Constantinople, acting as his personal bodyguards.

The eastern trade routes eventually led to Constantinople, capital city of the Byzantine empire (the eastern half of the old Roman empire). The Vikings called it Miklagard, which meant 'the great city'. It was a huge trading centre, with a population of a million people.

△ Constantinople was a beautiful city, famed for its bustling markets, fine churches and palaces. It was perfectly positioned to welcome traders from both Europe and Asia.

Life in the Viking world

Viking society consisted of kings, jarls (wealthy chieftains) and karls, ordinary Vikings who made up most of the population. There were also thralls, slaves who had been captured in raids or convicted of a crime. Life was hard for most people. Sick people who could not work were often simply left to die.

Viking life expectancy was 55 years at best. Most illnesses were treated with herbal remedies and magic, but serious diseases were usually fatal. The most common complaints were lice, fleas and stomach aches. These were caused by traces of poisonous weeds found in the bread grain.

▷ Rune stones were placed to claim ownership of a patch of land, or to commemorate a dead friend or relative. Runes were letters, made chiefly of straight lines.

The Viking judicial system was administered by the 'thing' assembly. This gathering of local land owners could last for weeks at a time. The assembly discussed local problems and settled arguments about theft, murder and land ownership.

△ Battle-wounded warriors were fed an onion and herb porridge. If the wound developed an onion odour, it was thought that the intestine had been pierced and that the victim would die.

The 'thing' dealt out swift and harsh punishments to anyone caught breaking the law. A thief, for instance, could expect to be hanged, and a suspected witch would die horribly through stoning, drowning or being sunk in a bog. Sometimes people could attempt to prove their innocence by completing an ordeal. This usually involved carrying red-hot iron or placing a hand in boiling water.

▽ Disagreements were often settled by a duel. Opponents faced one another on a small area marked out by a cloth. They used swords or axes, and had a shield for defence. Duels were usually fought to the death.

Quiz

Y ou've seen how the Vikings lived, traded, fought and explored. Now test your knowledge with this quiz. Answers can be found on page 32.

1. There were rune stones all over the Viking world. What were runes?

a) Pictures of warriors.

b) Letters in the Viking alphabet.

c) Sign posts.

2. Why were meat and fish salted during the summer months?

a) To preserve them so that they could be eaten during the winter.

b) To improve flavour – Vikings liked salty food.

c) To make them more tender.

3. What was a 'Berserker'?

a) A type of bear.

b) A fish stew.

c) A fierce warrior.

4. Why did people have to empty their drinking horn before putting it down?

a) Because it did not have a flat bottom, so the drink would spill out.

b) To show politeness – it was rude not to finish a drink.

c) So that they would be served some more.

5. What did the Viking expression 'game of iron' refer to?

a) It was the name that blacksmiths gave to their profession.

b) It was an expression for duels with double-handed swords.

c) It was the poetic phrase for a battle.

6. What was a 'jarl'?

a) It was a type of cheese particularly popular in Iceland.

b) It was the term used to describe a local chieftain.

c) It was a cooking pot used for making soup.

7. Of what was Frey the Norse god?

a) Frey was the god of war and fighting.

b) Frey was the god of wine and beer.

c) Frey was the god of nature and fertility.

8. What was 'hnefatafl'?

a) It was a board game that was similar to chess.

b) It was a club that was carried by the god Odin.

c) It was a wooden storage chest.

9. Why was Erik the Red, the Viking discoverer of Greenland, outlawed from Iceland?

a) He was accused of stealing sheep from a neighbouring farm.

b) He publicly insulted the local chieftain.

c) He committed manslaughter.

10. Who discovered Vinland?

a) Leif Eriksson.

b) Erik the Red.

c) Vik the Viking.

11. Why did Viking women cover their hair with a scarf?

a) As a sign of modesty.

b) To keep their hair tidy and out of their eyes.

c) To keep their heads warm in the cold winter months.

Index

Acknowledgements

Additional design
Mike Davis, Jane Tassie

Picture credits
b = bottom, c = centre, l = left, r = right, t = top
6tl The Bridgeman Art Library/University of Oslo, Norway; 8cl The Bridgeman Art Library/ Nationalmuseet, Copenhagen, Denmark; 12tr Werner Forman Archive/Statens Historiska Museum,

Stockholm; 17bc Werner Forman Archive/Statens Historiska Museum, Stockholm; 18bl Ancient Art & Architecture

The publisher would like to thank the following for permission to reproduce their material. Every care has been taken to trace copyright holders. However, if there have been unintentional omissions or failure to trace copyright holders, we apologize and will, if informed, endeavour to make corrections in any future edition.

Quiz answers

1 b) 2 a) 3 c) 4 a) 5 c) 6 b) 7 c) 8 a) 9 c) 10 a) 11 a)